Bigfoot Wallace

Bigfoot Wallace

By
Jo Harper

Illustrated by Virginia Roeder

EAKIN PRESS 🛡 Austin, Texas

For my friend Wayne Gunn,
an unfailing source
of scholarship and laughter
— JH

For Richard, who notices
all the details
— VR

FIRST EDITION

Copyright © 1999
By Jo Harper and Virginia Roeder

Published in the United States of America
By Eakin Press
A Division of Sunbelt Media, Inc.
P.O. Box 90159
Austin, TX 78709
email: eakinpub@sig.net
www.eakinpress.com

2 3 4 5 6 7 8 9

1-57168-223-6

Contents

1

Blowing in to Texas

William Alexander Wallace kicked into the world back in 1817 in Lexington, Virginia. He weighed in at thirteen pounds. He was a whopper. When he grew to be a man, he was six feet two inches tall and weighed 240 pounds. He was still a whopper. And he was strong, to boot, in body and in spirit.

Wallace learned to trail like a bloodhound and read signs like an Apache, but what he learned to do best was survive. He was one of the toughest men to ever hit Texas, and he lived to tell about things that some folks wither up just thinking about.

Wallace was picking apples in his daddy's orchard in Virginia, peaceful as you please, when word came that his brother and his cousin had been killed at Goliad. They had been fighting to free Texas from Mexico.

That was too much for Wallace. He couldn't stay on the peaceful farm anymore. He felt called on to do his duty. But before he could leave Virginia, the war was over.

He had missed out on fighting
Santa Anna. But just the same, he
struck out south and west, headed for
Texas. He was twenty-three years old
and strong. He figured there was some
way he could help out in the new
republic.

He traveled by way of New
Orleans on a schooner named *Diadem*.
His rifle, Sweet Lips, went with him.

A whale of a storm blew in. The
good ship *Diadem* rolled and tossed.
The passengers looked sick. They
turned green around the gills.

The storm got worse and worse.
The *Diadem* bucked and pitched like a
wild mustang. The folks on board
looked as if they had been pulled

through a knothole backwards. But
Wallace was perky as a bridegroom.

When the ship pulled into
Galveston, the passengers had to be
carried to solid land. Wallace helped
carry them.

Now in Texas, he was about to
start some real adventures.

2
A New Name

Wallace could swing a broadaxe steady and true. He got a job helping to build the city of Austin, the new capital of the Republic of Texas. While Wallace chopped and hewed, a Waco chief named Bigfoot was busy too— busy stealing the settlers' horses.

Chief Bigfoot left a mighty peculiar track. It was fourteen inches long, and the right big toe splayed to the side.

One night the Waco named Bigfoot prowled in the kitchen of a man named Garvis. Bigfoot left tracks behind which were bold and plain. They led straight to Wallace's house.

Garvis was ready to brand Wallace as a thief, but Wallace took off his right boot and put his foot in the right footprint. His foot was

big—but not that big. And his toe didn't stick out to the side.

Garvis apologized for suspecting an innocent man. After that, as a joke Wallace's pal William Fox started calling him Bigfoot. The name stuck. Far and wide, folks hailed him as Bigfoot Wallace.

3

Saved by the Flux

Bigfoot Wallace came close to getting hitched once in his life. He was engaged to be married. But a flux epidemic that hit Austin in the winter of 1839 changed those plans. Flux was similar to diarrhea.

This time Bigfoot Wallace was laid just as low as everybody else. He was knocking on death's door. Fortunately, an old French woman stayed with him and fed him small spoonfuls of mush. She saved his life. But all his thick, curly black hair fell out. He didn't feel comfortable going out in public, much less going to his own wedding.

Wallace went to Mount Bonnell, lived in a cave, and hunted bear. He waited for his hair to grow back. Every day he rubbed bear grease on his head, then washed it in the Colorado River.

While Bigfoot was waiting to look presentable, his friend William Fox came to visit him. He told Bigfoot that his sweet-heart had married someone else.

Bigfoot didn't let himself feel downhearted. He said, "I'm glad she's gone. I don't want a woman that can't wait until a man's hair grows out."

You could say that Bigfoot Wallace escaped matrimony by way of the flux.

4

A Crack at Santa Anna

In 1840 horse thieves and hooligans were hopping around San Antonio as thick as fleas. Captain Jack Hays raised a company of Texas Rangers to clean the place up.

To join the Rangers, a man had to be brave enough to look a growling bear in the eye without flinching. He had to ride fast enough to outrun a jackrabbit. And he had to be able to shoot a fly from fifty paces. He also had to have a gun and a horse worth one hundred dollars.

Bigfoot Wallace joined up.

He figured there would be plenty of hooligans to corral, but he didn't know he was going to get a crack at fighting Santa Anna after all.

In 1842, six years after Texas won its independence at the Battle of San Jacinto, Santa Anna sent the Mexican army to invade Texas again. The army hit San Antonio twice in a row, and the Mexican soldiers took some Texas citizens captive. Sam Houston called for volunteers to fight the Mexicans and bring back the captured Texans.

Ranger Bigfoot Wallace signed on. So did some other brave men.

Altogether, 700 riders, 1,200 horses and mules, and 500 cattle set out for Laredo under the command of General Somervell. They were in for a terrible journey.

5
Stuck in the Mud

General Somervell had the fool notion that the volunteers shouldn't follow the clear, well-worn Presidio Trail. Instead, he led them down the wild Laredo Trail. It was thick with chaparral bushes and mesquite grass. To call it a trail was a whopping exaggeration.

It was winter and the grass was

sparse and dry. The horses could hardly stay alive on it, and the brackish water was foul.

The volunteers got to the Nueces River on December 4, 1842, only to find that the water was high and raging. They stopped dead in their tracks. Then Captain Cameron, who hailed from Scotland, stood tall in his tartan plaid and shouted, "We'll bridge the stream!"

Cameron, Captain Hays, and Bigfoot Wallace rode their mounts into the cold water and swam across. They didn't seem to mind that it was a torrent.

Luckily for them, tall trees grew along the river. The men pulled axes

out of their saddlebags and started chopping. They chopped the trees so that they fell across the river. Then they formed the trees into a rough bridge. Now the other volunteers could cross the stream.

But that's when their luck ran out. After crossing the river, the volunteers found the land to be so soggy that they couldn't ride their horses. They could

18

barely even lead them. In two days
they made only five miles.

The Texans seemed trapped in
a nightmare. Men, mules, and horses
stretched out a mile, struggling through
water and mud. They floundered forward. The bog was swallowing their
animals. Many pack mules stuck fast
in the bog and had to be shot so they
wouldn't suffer a slow, painful death.

Wallace's big mule sank in a bog,
too, but he managed to get him out. He
slapped the mule's flanks while some
other volunteers pushed on his rump
and some tugged at his head. At last,
with a heave, the big mule lurched out.
The volunteers were so glad, they
whooped with laughter.

But they grumbled plenty too. Why had Somervell led them down such a fool trail?

When they got to firm ground, they pitched camp and ate supper. They were alive, and they were comrades. That deserved celebration, so they recited poetry around the campfire and had a good time.

6
Staying to Fight

They still had a long way to go. As they marched on toward Laredo, they caught a Mexican scout. Bigfoot had the job of guarding him. He sure didn't want to let his prisoner get away, so he stuck to him tight. He even slept with him so the scout couldn't sneak away at night.

But Bigfoot was tired—dog-tired.

He slept so hard, he didn't notice when the scout slipped a saddle under the blankets to take his place. And he sure didn't notice when the scout high-tailed it away from camp.

When Bigfoot awoke, his face was mighty red. It was downright embarrassing to let a prisoner outsmart you. Worse still, the expedition was now

22

messed up. The scout was gone, the beans were spilled, and the volunteers couldn't surprise the enemy.

When the Texans got to Laredo, it was deserted. They crossed the Rio Grande and went to the town of Guerrero. The *alcalde* (mayor) came out to meet the volunteers. He surrendered. He even promised to furnish supplies to the Texans, if they would only spare the citizens of the town.

The Texans were all just as dog-tired as Bigfoot Wallace. By now some volunteers were on foot because even the horses who made it through the bog had given out completely.

The *alcalde*'s offer sounded good to them. They agreed to not harm the

citizens if the town would give them
500 beeves and $5,000.

When the Texans went to claim
the supplies and money, they found
that the *rancheros* had driven all the
livestock out of town. They were long
gone, and the villagers had only a few
mules with ragged saddle blankets and
$173 to give to the hungry Texans.

The Texans just about lost their
sense of humor. To top it off, they
heard that General Pedro de Ampudia
was headed their way with a large
Mexican force.

General Somervell decided to
throw in the towel without even trying
to get the Texan captives back. He
said, "All who wish to march north

with me, step forward ten paces. We will leave at once."

Two hundred men stepped forward to go with Somervell. They felt that they couldn't fight without supplies.

But 303 volunteers stood firm. One of them was Bigfoot Wallace. He and the other volunteers who decided to stick it out elected William S. Fisher as their colonel. Fisher knew the language and the country. And he was a good soldier.

7
A Fancy Hostage

The Rio Grande was high, but the volunteers found some Mexican barges. They used the barges to cross to the Mexican side.

On December 23 they pitched camp near the town of Mier and sent some men to demand provisions. The *alcalde* gave them his word that food and other supplies would be delivered the next day. This time the Texans wouldn't take anyone's word. They took the *alcalde* back to camp as a hostage until the goods came.

The well-groomed *alcalde* had on a fancy uniform and carried a silver-headed cane with silk tassels. He looked out of place with the ragged Texans. The *alcalde* expected to be offered a good meal and a tent, but he found out that the Texans had only a few slabs of meat to share with him. He also found out that they just threw themselves on the ground to sleep. He had to sleep that way too.

The volunteers didn't want the *alcalde* to escape the way Bigfoot's scout had. He had to sleep with Tom

Green—with his leg between Green's legs, that is.

Two days passed. The Texans were out of food. No supplies came. On Christmas morning they captured a Mexican and found out that General Pedro de Ampudia was occupying Mier. The general had seized their supplies. They also found out that General Canales and his troops had joined Ampudia.

The Texans decided to cross over and fight.

8
"To Your Stones"

Three hundred and three volunteers against the Mexican forces seemed like a few gnats against a whole herd of cattle. Also, the Texans would be fighting in a town they didn't know.

The volunteers decided to let the Mexicans fire first. They would jump out and shoot while the Mexicans reloaded.

30

The Texans first picked off the gunners. Dodging cannon balls, they took shelter in the houses around the plaza. Then they fought from house to house and shot from the rooftops. Ammunition was scarce. They had to make every bullet count.

Captain Cameron, still in his tartan plaid and with a Bowie knife in his belt, ordered his men to grab stones from the wall and yard. When their ammunition ran out, he shouted, "Boys, to your stones!"

The Texans hurled the rocks. They not only smashed heads, but they also confounded the enemy. Their actions bought them a little

time. But many of their men lay dead
or wounded.

9

Into a Corral

The Mexicans came with a white flag and offered a kind of truce. They promised that the captives would be treated as prisoners of war. General Fisher decided to accept the offer.

Bigfoot Wallace knew that the truce was just a trick. He told the other Texans so. Cameron agreed with Bigfoot, and his troops did too.

But the other Texans didn't.

Finally, Cameron said, "Boys, it is no use to continue the fight any longer. We will have to knock under."

Wallace was still against calling it quits. He was the last man to give up his gun.

The Texan captives had to march from Mier to a ranch outside Camargo. It was a hard twenty-five miles, and a norther was blowing. When they arrived at the ranch, there wasn't a building big enough to hold the Texans. They were placed in a corral.

The Texans believed in making the best of a bad situation. They dropped down on their hands and

knees and pawed the ground. They
bellowed like bulls.

The
Mexicans
were bum-
fuzzled.
Finally, they
realized that
the Texans
weren't
crazy, just
goofy. They
laughed at
the joke.

10

Escape!

Bigfoot Wallace had a long shirt that went down to his knees. It was a good thing he did, because his pants wore out.

In Matamoros, the Texans were given clothes. They had a week of shelter and rest. Then Santa Anna ordered his generals to march them all the way to Mexico City in chains.

General Canales was to take charge of the Texans.

The Texans kicked up a fuss. General Ampudia told them he was sick about Santa Anna's command. He had stayed awake all night thinking about it, but there was nothing he could do.

General Ampudia did manage to help the Texans a little. He ordered that their chains be removed. General Canales let the order stand—for a while.

Bigfoot's friend Captain Cameron cooked up a scheme to make a get-away. Just before sunrise on February 11, 1843, Cameron raised his hat. "Well, boys, we'll go it!"

The 193 Texans charged the guards. They grabbed guns and ammunition. They took the horses and mules that the Mexicans had saddled for the morning journey, and headed north. Eighteen men had fallen, dead or wounded.

11

A Big Drink

The Texans made a great escape, but they made the mistake of going toward the mountains. Then they were in a mess.

They wandered without water for six days. Their tongues were so parched and swollen that they couldn't close their mouths. They scratched in the shade of bushes trying to find cool earth to put on their throats and stomachs.

Some Mexican cavalrymen rounded them up. They were afraid the Texans would kill themselves if they drank too much water all at once, so they gave water to them a little at a time.

Bigfoot noticed a horseman who had a big water gourd. It was Bigfoot's own gourd that had been taken from him at Mier. He said in Spanish, "That is my gourd. Give it up."

The Mexican soldier said, "*Probrecito,*" and handed the gourd to him. Bigfoot started guzzling water.

Another Texan, Tom Davis, ran up to him and said, "Give me some, Foot."

Wallace answered that he couldn't turn it loose. Davis tried to pull the gourd away from Bigfoot's mouth, but he couldn't.

A Mexican officer said, "Take that away. He'll kill himself."

Several soldiers tried to take it away, but they couldn't. Bigfoot was too tall.

He drank a gallon of water and fell down in a dead sleep. He didn't move all night, and the soldiers thought he'd never wake up again. But the next day he was fit as a fiddle.

42

12
The Lucky Bean

The Mexicans made the Texans march to Salado. There, General Santa Anna ordered that every tenth Texan was to be shot.

The Texans were chained together in pairs and ordered to draw beans from a pitcher. One hundred fifty-nine white beans and seventeen black beans were in the pitcher. The black beans were death beans.

Bigfoot Wallace was one of the last men to draw. He had noticed that the black beans were a little larger than the white ones. When it came his turn, he squeezed his huge hand down into the narrow pitcher neck, got two beans in his hand, and felt them. Then he pulled out the smaller one. It was a white bean.

Bigfoot was lucky, but seventeen brave Texas volunteers were not lucky. They were lined up and shot.

Captain Cameron had drawn a white bean too. But the Mexican leaders hated him as a troublemaker, so they decided to shoot him anyway.

44

The guards tied Cameron's hands behind him and started to blindfold his eyes. "No!" he shouted, taking off the blindfold. "Ewen Cameron can now, as he has often done before, for the liberty of Texas look death in the face without winking!" Then he gave his last command. "Fire!"

Cameron had given the Mexican guards an order that ended his own life.

13
Stalling and Clowning

The surviving Texans began a thousand-mile march to Mexico City. It took four hard months. When they arrived they were given prison uniforms and put to work.

The Texans joked about how they looked in their bright red and green prison stripes. They planned to do as little work as possible.

To get even, the guards started hitching the strongest men to wagons. Of course, Bigfoot Wallace was one of the strongest. One day he grabbed a cart, neighed like a horse, and galloped down the hill. Mexican guards shouted at him, but he hurtled right along. When he reached a curve, he let the wagon go. It wrecked.

Bigfoot expected to be punished, but the guards laughed at his tomfoolery. Santa Anna didn't laugh. He sent the Texans to the most dreaded prison in Mexico—the Castle of Perote.

48

14
Keeping Up Spirits

In the Castle of Perote, the Texans slept on bare floors. There was only one blanket for every ten men. They had to wear chains all the time. That didn't get them down, though.

When the guards put the chains on the Texans, the Texans thanked them and acted like it was a big favor. They called the chains their "jewelry."

The Mexicans didn't know that the prisoners had figured out how to get out of their chains at night.

The Texans didn't mind the work or the chains too much. They didn't fuss about being cold and having no beds. But they hated having to act humble and take off their hats when the governor passed. They'd sooner take a licking with a cane.

The rambunctious, happy-go-lucky Bigfoot wasn't about to let Santa Anna steal his good spirits. Neither were the other Texans. They were tormented with body lice, so they had louse races. When a favorite louse got ahead, they cheered. When it fell behind, they groaned.

Some of the Texans managed to make fiddles. Some- times they danced, shaking their legs and stepping lively on their sore, swollen feet.

15
A Hard Trip Home

At last, the United States intervened on behalf of the Republic of Texas. On September 16, 1844, the Mexican government gave each of the last surviving 120 volunteers a dollar and set them free.

The Texans had been in prison for more than a year, and they had been away from home for two years. It was good to be free, but they wondered how they could make it 2,000 miles on foot with just one dollar. It looked hopeless, but they headed out.

They hadn't gone far when they were stopped by robbers on horseback. Bigfoot told them he wasn't exactly loaded with money, and he showed them his passport, signed

by Santa Anna. The robbers called
Santa Anna a scoundrel and told the
Texans they should have killed him.
Bigfoot agreed with that.

The Mexican robbers and the
Texans became friends. The robbers
took them to a big ranch, and gave
them food and hospitality.

The Texans made it to Vera Cruz.
A yellow fever epidemic was raging.
People were dying by the hundreds.
The Texans had to wait eleven days
before they could find a ship bound for
New Orleans, but the one they found
had been infected with yellow fever.
The Texans were willing to risk it, just
to get home.

Bigfoot Wallace was weak from

TEXAS
RIO GRANDE
NUECES RIVER
SAN ANTONIO
LAREDO
GUERRERO
MIER
CAMARGO
MATAMOROS
MEXICO
GULF
OF
MEXICO
SALADO
MEXICO CITY
PEROTE
VERACRUZ
TO NEW ORLEANS

the hard two years. He fell sick with yellow fever, just like everyone else. The ship captain, a Frenchman, gave Bigfoot a concoction of castor oil and bitter red roots. It worked. Bigfoot survived.

That was the second time a French person saved his life.

16
Still a Fighter

The Mier expedition was the
longest and roughest adventure
Bigfoot Wallace ever experienced. He
was plenty glad when he arrived back
home in Texas.

He didn't kick back and take it
easy, though. There was still a heap of
work to do in Texas. He worked as a
ranger, as a tracker, and as an Indian

fighter. He could track a runaway prisoner or a lost child when everyone else thought it was hopeless.

Once Bigfoot and some friends were trailing Indians. The Indians figured out that they were being followed. They set up an ambush.

Bigfoot was riding along the trail when an Indian appeared in front of him. The Indian's gun was aimed at Bigfoot's chest.

It seemed like "lights out" time for sure, but Bigfoot thought fast. He threw himself backward off his horse, and landed with his gun drawn and ready. The Indian's bullet had gone over his head, and Bigfoot shot the Indian.

17
Twenty-Seven Eggs

In 1850 Bigfoot began carrying the mail by stagecoach from San Antonio to El Paso. That was 600 miles of Indian country.

Bigfoot took six mounted guards with him. They rode close to the rear of the stage. He took extra mules too.

On one trip Bigfoot went twenty-four hours without eating. When he stopped at a cafe near El Paso, the owner said that breakfast

cost only twenty-five cents. Bigfoot
ordered twenty-seven eggs. When the
cafe owner looked downhearted,
Bigfoot laughed and handed him
a dollar.

The twenty-seven eggs were
almost more than Bigfoot could
manage, but he made it. Twenty-seven
eggs couldn't stump a man who
claimed to have eaten every critter in
Texas—including skunk.

18
Stagecoach Defender

One night, Bigfoot noticed that the mules were uneasy. He saw smoke signals in the distance. He was sure that Indians were going to try to capture the stagecoach.

Bigfoot camped in an open glade with short grass. The men who rode with him bedded down with their guns beside them.

The
night
was
still
except for
the soft   sound of
mules cropping   grass. Then a
raven flushed up   from the
chaparral, and lighted on a guard's head.
The guard thought the raven was an

64

omen. He asked Bigfoot what it meant.

Bigfoot said, "It means that the Comanches are in that chaparral brush over there. They scared that raven off his roost, and he mistook your head for a stump."

Bigfoot knew he was right because he had one mule that never would eat when Indians were around. That mule wasn't eating. It was pacing and snorting. Bigfoot said, "They're here, boys. Handle your guns."

But the Comanches didn't come. In a few hours the men began to relax. A guard named Peter Weble stretched out full length on his back and rested his head between two wheel spokes on the stagecoach.

Wallace stayed alert and as still as stone. When three shapes darted out of the brush and toward the camp, he commanded, "Nip 'em, quick!"

The Indians knew they were discovered. War whoops rang out. Arrows flew. Guns fired. But soon the Texans heard a different kind of commotion.

Peter Weble had fallen sound asleep. When the fighting started, he jerked awake and wedged his head in the spokes—tight. As Weble struggled, the stage rattled and rocked. He managed to get out, but his neck was sore for two weeks. Bigfoot said he had worried that Weble would run off and carry the stagecoach with him!

19
Legend of a Hero

Bigfoot Wallace was a legend in his own time. So, of course, folks started making up stories about him. Bigfoot wasn't one to be left out of the fun, so he made up a few himself.

He claimed that after his sweetheart left him, he gave up romance. He said that when he was in Mexico, bound with his hands tied behind him, an old Mexican woman made faces at him. He bit her on the neck. And that, he said, was the closest he ever came to kissing a woman.

Bigfoot Wallace was stronger than a team of mules, braver than a brace of bears, and tougher than a boot heel wrapped in rawhide. That's not a legend. It's a natural fact, straight from the mule's mouth.

Wallace died of natural causes at the age of eighty-one in Devine, Texas. He was buried in an unmarked grave. That didn't set well with Texans. They thought Bigfoot deserved to be buried like a hero. Later his body was exhumed and reburied in the State

Cemetery in Austin. His headstone reads:

BIGFOOT WALLACE

Here Lies He Who

Spent His

Manhood

Defending the

Homes of Texas

Brave, Honest

and Faithful

Born

April 3, 1817

Died

January 7, 1899

Works Consulted

Bartlett, Robert M. *Those Valiant Texans—A Breed Apart.* Portsmouth, NH: Peter E. Randall Publisher, 1989.

Bell, Thomas W. *A Narrative of the Capture and Subsequent Sufferings of the Mier Prisoners.* 1845. Waco: Texian Press, 1964.

Caldecott, Wilfred H. *Santa Anna, The Story of the Enigma Who Once was Mexico.* Norman: University of Oklahoma Press, 1936.

Day, James M. *Black Beans and Goose Quills, Literature of the Texan Mier Expedition.* Waco: Texian Press, 1970.

Duval, John C. *Big-Foot Wallace, The Texas Ranger and Hunter.* Southern District of Georgia: J. W. Burke & Co., 1870.

Fehrenbach, T. R. *Fire and Blood: A History of Mexico.* New York: Macmillan Press, 1973.

———. *Lone Star: A History of Texas and the Texans.* New York: Macmillan Press, 1980.

Haynes, Sam W. *Soldiers of Misfortune, The Somervell and Mier Expeditions.* Austin: University of Texas Press, 1990.

Hunter, John Warren. *Adventures of a Mier Prisoner: Being the Thrilling Experiences of John Rufus Alexander, Who Was With the Ill-Fated Expedition Which Invaded Mexico.* Bandera: Frontier Times, n.d.

Iglehart, Fanny Chambers Gooch. *The Boy Captive of the Texas Mier Expedition.* J. R. Wood, 1909.

71

Jenkins, John Holland. *Recollections of Early Texas: The Memories of John Holland Jenkins*. Edited by John Holmes Jenkins III. Austin: University of Texas Press, 1958.

Lane, Walter P. *The Adventures and Recollections of a San Jacinto Veteran*. Marshall: Tri-Weekly Herald, 1887.

McCutchan, Joseph D. *Mier Expedition Diary: A Texas Prisoner's Account*. Edited by Joseph Milton Nance. Austin: University of Texas Press, 1978.

Morrell, Zenos N. *Flowers and Fruits in the Wilderness*. Waco: Baylor University Press, 1976.

Nance, Joseph Milton. *Dare-Devils All: Texas Mier Expedition, 1842–1844*. Austin: Eakin Press, 1998.

———. *Attack and Counter-Attack, The Texas-Mexican Frontier, 1842*. Austin: University of Texas Press, 1964.

Newcomb, W. W., Jr. *The Indians of Texas*. Austin: University of Texas Press, 1961.

O'Brien, Steven. *Antonio Lopez De Santa Anna*. New York: Chelsea House, 1992.

Rittenhouse, J. D. *Maverick Tales, True Stories of Early Texas*. New York: Winchester Press, 1971.

Smithwick, Noah. *The Evolution of a State or Recollections of Old Texas Days*. Austin: University of Texas Press, 1984.

Sowell, Andrew Jackson. *Life of "Bigfoot" Wallace*. Austin: Steck, 1957. (Facsimile reproduction of the original 1899 edition.)

Thompson, Waddy. *Recollections of Mexico*. New York: Wiley and Putnam, 1846.

Walker, Samuel. *Samuel Walker's Account of the Mier Expedition*. Edited by Marilyn McAdams Sibley. Austin: Texas State Historical Association, 1978.

Webb, Walter Prescott. *The Texas Rangers, A Century of Frontier Defense*. Austin: University of Texas Press, 1965.

Wright, Muriel H. *A Guide to the Indian Tribes of Oklahoma*. Norman: University of Oklahoma Press, 1951.

	DATE DUE		